T0055368

SCHIRMER'S LIBRARY OF MUSICAL CLASSICS

DOMENICO SCARLATTI

Sixty Sonatas

In Two Volumes

Edited in Chronological Order
from the Manuscript and Earliest Printed Sources
with a Preface
by
RALPH KIRKPATRICK

Volume I - Library Vol. 1774
➔ Volume II - Library Vol. 1775

ISBN 0-7935-4396-7

G. SCHIRMER, Inc.

DISTRIBUTED BY

HAL•LEONARD
CORPORATION
7777 W. BLUEMOUND RD. P.O. BOX 13819 MILWAUKEE, WI 53213

CONTENTS

VOLUME I

CONTENTS (*Continued*)

Sonata XXXI (K. 263) in Venice IV

Sonata XLI (K. 420) in Parma XI

iv

Sonata XLVI (K. 461) in Venice XI

Sonata LX (K. 545) in Parma XV

Sixty Sonatas

Edited by Ralph Kirkpatrick

Domenico Scarlatti

K. 263
Venice IV 28, Parma VI 19
Longo 321

41

44

47

50

53

56

K. 264
Venice IV 29, Parma VI 20
Longo 466

XXXII

121

131

141

151

161

171

K. 308
Venice VI 13, Parma VIII 7
Longo 359

Cantabile

XXXIII

36

41

46

51

55

60

K. 309
Venice VI 14, Parma VIII 8
Longo 454

Allegro

XXXIV

52

57

62

67

72

K. 366
Venice VIII 9, Parma X 6
Longo 119

K. 367
Venice VIII 10, Parma X 7
Longo 172

42917

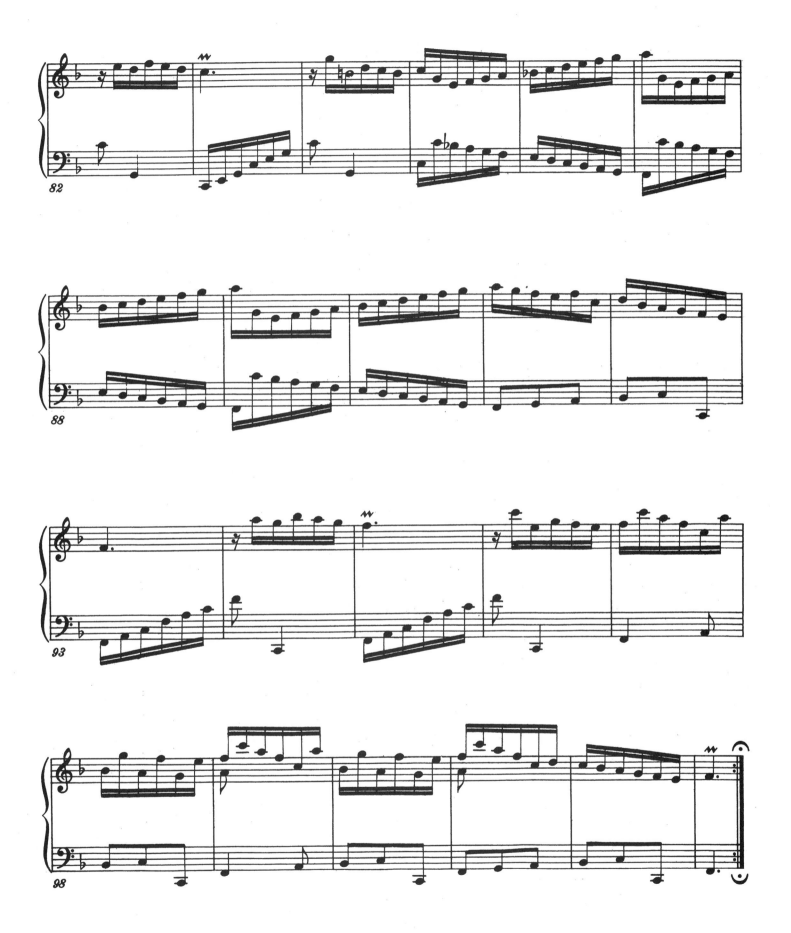

K. 394
Venice IX 7, Parma XI 7
Longo 275

K. 395
Venice IX 8, Parma XI 8
Longo 65

33

39

45

51

58

65

71

78

86

94

103

109

115

122

131

K. 402
Venice IX 15, Parma XI 15
Longo 427

K. 403
Venice IX 16, Parma XI 16
Longo 470

87

93

99

105

111

K. 420
Venice X 3, Parma XI 29
Longo S. 2

42917

42917

44

K. 421
Venice X 4, Parma XI 30
Longo 252

107

113

119

125

131

137

K. 426
Venice X 9, Parma XII 16
Longo 128

XLIII

90

99

108

116

125

134

K. 427
Venice X 10, Parma XII 17
Longo 286

Presto, quanto sia possibile

XLIV

K. 460
Venice XI 7, Parma XIII 7
Longo 324

Allegro

XLV

56

60

65

70

42917

K. 461
Venice XI 8, Parma XIII 8
Longo 8

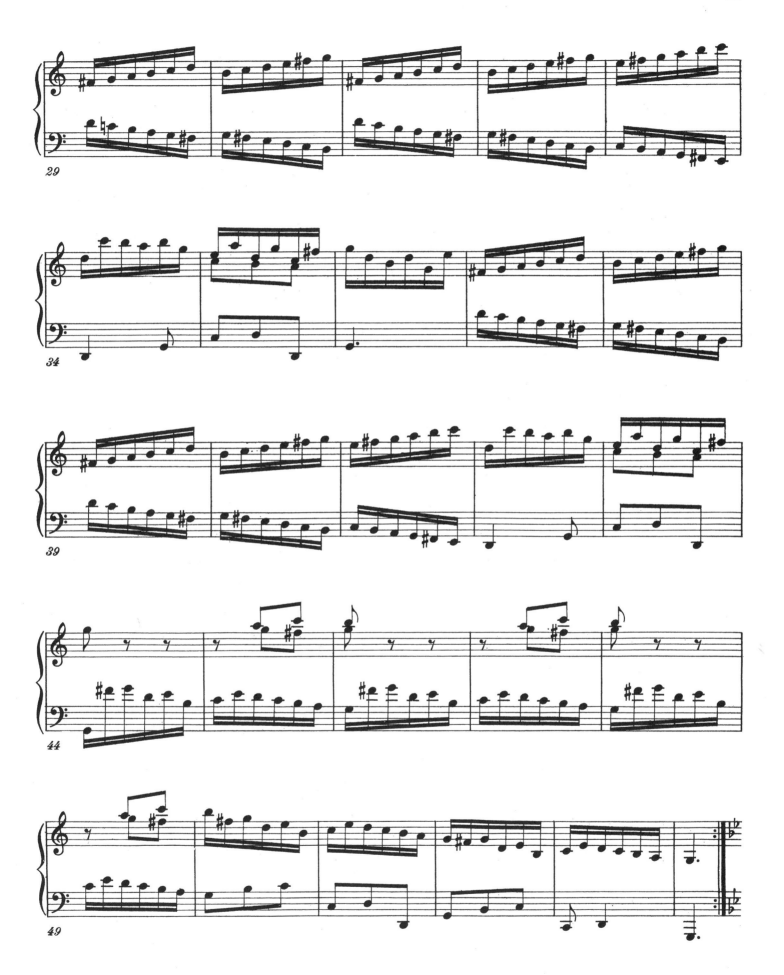

55

62

69

76

83

90

97

104

110

116

122

128

K. 470
Venice XI 17, Parma XIII 17
Longo 304

K. 471
Venice XI 18, Parma XIII 18
Longo 82

XLVIII

K. 490
Venice XII 7, Parma XIV 7
Longo 206

42917

42917

K. 491
Venice XII 8, Parma XIV 8
Longo 164

K. 492
Venice XII 9, Parma XIV 9
Longo 14

K. 493
Venice XII 10, Parma XIV 10
Longo S. 24

Allegro

LII

42917

K. 494
Venice XII 11, Parma XIV 11
Longo 287

59

64

69

73

78

83

88

94

99

104

109

115

42917

K. 513
Venice XII 30, Parma XIV 30
Longo S. 3

Pastorale
Moderato

Molto allegro

Presto

36

41

46

52

K. 516
Venice XIII 3, Parma XV 4
Longo S. 12

Allegretto

LV

52

63

73

83

92

133

141

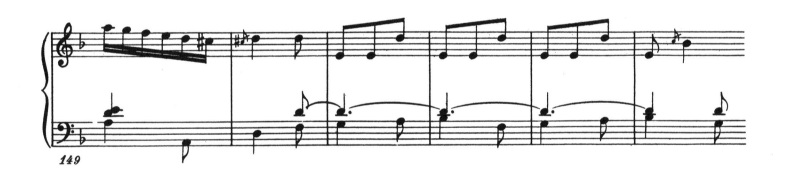

149

155

42917

K. 517
Venice XIII 4, Parma XV 3
Longo 266

Prestissimo

LVI

42917

K. 518
Venice XIII 5, Parma XV 5
Longo 116

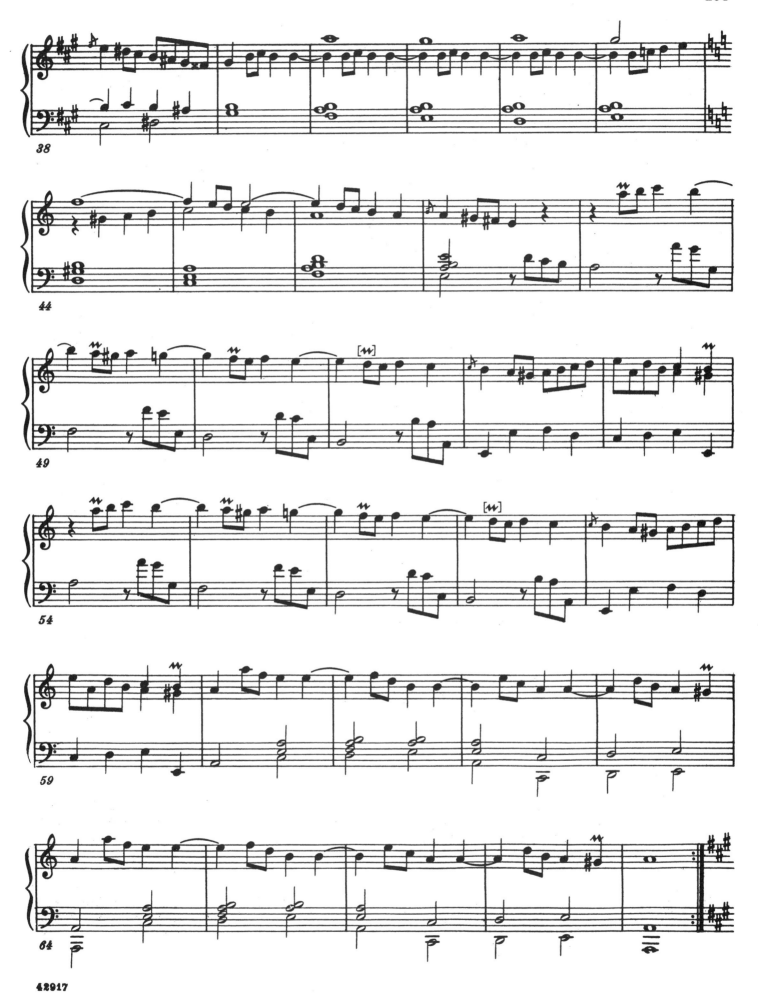

42917

K. 519
Venice XIII 6, Parma XV 6
Longo 475

Allegro assai

LVIII

94

104

114

124

K. 544
Parma XV 31
Longo 497

K. 545
Parma XV 32
Longo 500

Prestissimo

LX

TEXT REVISION

This edition is drawn from the closest known sources to Scarlatti's originals. No keyboard autographs of Scarlatti are known to be extant. The abbreviated references cited in connection with each sonata may be explained as follows.

SOURCES AND NUMBERING OF THE SONATAS

1. *Essercizi.* *Essercizi per Gravicembalo*, an engraved volume of thirty sonatas published in 1738 at Scarlatti's instigation.

2. *Venice.* Fifteen manuscript volumes of sonatas copied out in Spain for Scarlatti's patroness and pupil, Queen Maria Barbara. Two unnumbered volumes are dated respectively 1742 (to this volume I refer as Venice XIV) and 1749 (to this I refer as Venice XV). The remaining volumes are numbered from I to XIII and dated from 1752 to 1757. The whole collection contains four hundred and ninety-six sonatas. Venice, Biblioteca Nazionale Marciana, MSS 9770-9784.

3. *Parma.* Fifteen manuscript volumes containing four hundred and sixty-three sonatas, also copied out in Spain and dated from 1752 to 1757. These volumes mostly duplicate the contents of the Venice series, and are largely in the same hand as its later volumes. Parma, Biblioteca Palatina, Sezione Musicale, now housed in the Conservatorio Arrigo Boito, A G 31406-31420.

4. *Worgan.* A Spanish manuscript volume containing forty-four sonatas, roughly contemporary with Venice XV, and once the property of Dr. John Worgan. London, British Museum, Add. 31553.

5. *Fitzwilliam.* A later Spanish manuscript volume containing twenty-four sonatas. Cambridge, Fitzwilliam Museum, 32 F 13.

Further particulars regarding these and additional sources of Scarlatti sonatas can be found in my *Domenico Scarlatti* (Princeton University Press, 1953), in Chapter VIII, Appendix V, and in its Catalogue of Scarlatti Sonatas.

In this edition the sonata numbers preceded by the letter K refer to the chronological numbering adopted in that catalogue.

Sonata numbers preceded by the name Longo refer to the arbitrary order in which five hundred and forty-five of the sonatas were published in Alessandro Longo's edition, *Opere Complete per Clavicembalo di Domenico Scarlatti* (Milan, Ricordi, [1906 ff.]).

The Venice and Parma manuscripts are of almost equal authenticity and show considerable evidence of having been copied from the same source, largely by the same copyists. There are however occasional slight variants between them, among which I have chosen what seems to me the most correct and most complete reading. In numerous cases the small omissions or mistakes of one manuscript are supplemented or corrected by the other. The Worgan manuscript in most cases is of less importance, but I have drawn from it a few small details that do not appear in the Venice and Parma manuscripts, although in a few cases I have tacitly rejected some of its additional ornaments and small variants when they appeared to me patently inferior. In this edition I have had occasion to use the Fitzwilliam manuscript only for Sonatas XIX and XX in order to confirm my choices among the slight variants of Venice and Parma readings.

Editorial Policy

With respect to the small variants among sources, my text represents a composite reading. I have not attempted in principle to give an accounting of all variants among manuscripts. This is not a variorum edition, but an attempt to choose the most complete and authoritative text. I have cited variants only when they offer to the performer a legitimate alternative to the reading I have chosen, when they explain my choices where there is room for doubt, or when they throw light on the general practices of Scarlatti's copyists. Mistakes or omissions unanimously committed by all the main sources are silently corrected when there is no room for doubt. When there is room for doubt about the manner of their emendation, my corrections are made recognizable in the text as editor's additions, or are mentioned in the text revision.

Doubtful accidentals are inserted above or below the note, or mentioned in the text revision. Where omitted accidentals are justified beyond a doubt, I have inserted them in the text without comment.

Ties not authenticated by any one source are indicated by dotted lines. I have adopted slurs, including those for appoggiaturas, only when they are present in one of the sources, and I have made no attempt to supplement them, even in dotted lines. Their use in the originals is too inconsistent. Similarly, in the rare instances of staccato markings, I have made no attempt at supplementing them.

The numerous missing ornaments that I have added are all enclosed in brackets. In a few cases I have been obliged to add missing notes. These are always enclosed in brackets or mentioned in the text revision. I have held these additions to what to me seemed the minimum required for the presentation of a complete text. There remain, however, passages whose inconsistency (unless conceivably intentional) may justify the individual player in adding notes, ties, or ornaments drawn from parallel passages.

Transcription into modern keyboard notation has necessitated a redistribution of the notes among the staves, and a rearrangement of stems. It will be noticed in the accompanying facsimiles that Scarlatti's copyists made every attempt to avoid the use of leger lines, so that notes for one hand were often divided between the staves; and that they had a tendency to crowd adjacent notes onto one staff, whether or not they were for one or two hands. In my text I have nearly always allocated notes to be played by the right hand to the upper staff, and those to be played by the left to the lower. The principal exceptions are represented by continuous passages moving from one staff to another, in which I have retained the sometimes ambiguous disposition of the original. In all cases, however, I have reproduced Scarlatti's own indications for the disposition of the hands, even when rendered unnecessary by my distribution of notes on the staves. (Scarlatti's original indications, M for "*manca*" and D for "*destra*" have been translated into L for "left" and R for "right.") In this way many seemingly arbitrary and unnecessarily difficult dispositions of hands may be seen to reflect Scarlatti's express intentions. In numerous cases, however, in which Scarlatti has not expressly indicated the disposition of notes among the hands, I have been obliged to make my own choice. This choice has been based on negotiability and musical clarity. (In Sonata VI, however, Scarlatti's own indications do not excel for negotiability or clarity. He leaves the ends of both halves of the sonata without express indications. In assigning the inverted dispositions of measures 45-50 and 85-88 in a manner that seems to reflect his intentions, I have perhaps been overfaithful to the perversity of his humor.)

As the facsimiles demonstrate, it was customary in Scarlatti's time to give separate stems to the individual notes of chords. In redistributing the notes on two staves and in clarifying part-writing, it has been necessary frequently to make my own decisions with respect to the direction of the stems and to the grouping on the stems of notes in chord passages. My basic principle has been to distinguish by separate stems and beams those passages that consistently present two or more melodic lines, even when they are merely octave doublings. In the frequent cases where inner parts appear and drop out without representing a consistent line, I have separated the outer voices of Scarlatti's two-voice skeleton, and have lumped the inner voices on stems in the opposite direction, thus leaving the soprano and bass lines clear. In left-hand passages, for example, I have used downward stems for the bass, and upward stems for the remaining voices. A very few exceptions have been dictated by considerations of musical clarity. Occasion-

ally a unison passage noted thus ♪♪♪♪ has been silently transcribed as ♪♪♪♪♪ in accord with the obvious musical context (as in Sonata V, measures 29 and 78). In a few cases I have added dotted lines to clarify part-writing.

I have retained the inexact notation of dotted rhythms that was so common in the 18th century. (See for example Sonata X, measure 58, etc.; and Sonata XXVII.)

The redistribution of notes between the staves has often necessitated the omission or addition of rests. As may be seen from the facsimiles, Scarlatti's copyists generally preferred empty spaces to the employment of rests during pauses. (The only rests occurring in Sonata VI, for example, are those before the last three sixteenths in measures 1, 6, and 50, and before the last eighth in measure 21 and 62.) I have inserted rests throughout this edition where they appeared to aid the modern eye, but I have not felt it necessary to encumber the text by enclosing them in brackets. It must be understood however that Scarlatti is often inconsistent in indicating the duration of notes before pauses, that notes may occasionally be partly prolonged through my inserted rests in the same way that notes outlining broken arpeggios may be held beyond their written value. At all times, however, the player's musical judgment should guide him in the observance of rests, in the same manner that a pianist's musical judgment determines his use of the damper pedal.

Key signatures have been modernized. Frequently, but not always, Scarlatti's copyists used one less accidental than we do in the signatures of minor keys (Sonatas XI, XII, XV, XVI, XXVII, XXVIII, XLIII, LV, LVI, LVIII) and of some major keys (Sonatas V, VIII, X, XXIII, XXIV, XXXVIII, XL).

The abbreviations of tempo indications have been written out in full, and occasional obsolete Italian spellings have been modernized.

The meaning of the corona at the double bar or at the end of many a sonata is not always clear. (See for example the double bar of Sonata IV.) In many cases it obviously represents an orthographical convention, a calligraphic ornament, and not an indication for prolonging a note or a pause. Moreover, coronas are often incompletely or inconsistently indicated in the manuscripts. Whenever they occur in one of the principal sources I reproduce them, leaving to the player the choice of regarding or disregarding them. Where a single corona obviously applies to both hands I have doubled it.

I have omitted the calligraphic slurs that appear at the double bar of many a sonata, since they might be interpreted by the modern performer as ties between the first and second halves (Sonatas XXXV, XXXVIII, XLV, LI, LII, LIII, LVI).

The notation of trills is not always consistent in the manuscript. It is clear that *tr* and ∿ were used interchangeably. For Sonatas I to XX I use *tr*, which is the notation of their sources, namely, *Essercizi*, Venice XIV and XV, and Worgan. The use of a dot *tr.* after the abbreviation is so inconsistent that I have disregarded it throughout. In Venice I-XIII and in Parma ∿ is predominant; *tr* appears only rarely, generally in connection with an inner voice. Therefore in Sonatas XXI to LX I use ∿ except for the few cases in which only *tr* is used. In the manuscripts the sign varies slightly, but it generally looks like this ∿ . I have translated it throughout as ∿ .

While it cannot definitely be established that *tr* is always an abbreviation for *Tremulo,* Sonata XVII (measures 56-60) provides some evidence to that effect. Sonata XXI (measures 25-32) however maintains a puzzlingly consistent distinction between *tremulo* and *tr* or ∿ .

The wavy line indicating the prolongation of a note beyond its written value (Sonata XII, for example) should not be confused with the sign for the trill. Occasionally a note prolonged in this fashion in one source can be found written out to its full duration in another. In such cases I have adopted the latter notation.

The notation of the time value of appoggiaturas varies among sources and is frequently inconsistent within the same text. Repeatedly the same appoggiatura can be found written as 𝅘𝅥𝅯 , 𝅘𝅥𝅮 , 𝅘𝅥𝅮 , or even 𝅘𝅥𝅰 , 𝅘𝅥𝅮 , or 𝅘𝅥 ! It is obvious that in such cases, as in most, the written value of the appoggiatura has little to do with the manner of its execution. I would have felt justified in reducing all the appoggiaturas of this edition to a uniform notation, were it not for the presence in later sonatas of a differentiation of note values that might reflect some kind of intention, even if not consistent or directly indicative of execution. As it is, I have adopted the exact notation of the *Essercizi* and of Venice, except for Sonatas XXV, XXIX, XXXI-XXXIV, XXXVII, XLII, L-LI, and LVI, in which I have followed the notation of Parma because of its slightly greater consistency. When appoggiaturas have been taken from a supplementary source I have generally retained their original notation, but in a few cases in which the notation (either Venice or Parma) that I am following is reasonably consistent, I have adapted the supplementary appoggiaturas to that notation. (I could have achieved a greater visual consistency in my text by combining sources for the notation of appoggiaturas, but the result would have given the deceptive impression of a regularity that in this respect none of the sources possesses.)

I have inserted measure numbers at the beginning of each brace. Their occasional divergence from those of Longo's edition may be explained as follows:

Sonata VIII: An extra measure is mistakenly inserted by Longo after measure 121.

Sonata X: Measure 81 of my text is omitted by Longo.

Sonata XI: I give a full measure to the second ending of the first half, whereas Longo elides it with the beginning of the second half. Thus my measure 32 is not present in Longo.

Sonata XIV: Measures 61-63 of my text are omitted by Longo.

Sonata XLV: Longo's use of a first and second ending at the end adds one more measure to his text than mine.

Sonata LX: Measures 14 and 18 of my text are omitted by Longo.

These are the only variants between my edition and Longo's that I have thought it necessary to mention. The numerous remaining discrepancies between his text and mine can be explained by my adherence to the sources cited.

NOTES ON THE TEXT OF THE SONATAS

SONATA I:

Variants are to be found in Venice XIV 31. They include extra bars which in my opinion do not represent an improvement on the *Essercizi* text, and additional trills which represent only a small portion of those that might well be introduced by an intelligent player.

Measures 44 and 86: I draw however from Venice XIV 31 the basses, which are missing in the *Essercizi*.

SONATA II:

Measures 3 and 5: Although the *Essercizi* places these trills above the right hand, parallel passages would seem to indicate that they apply to the left. I have so placed them.

Measures 77, 79, 84, 86: The *Essercizi* places the trills before the alto, but I have interpreted them as applying to the soprano.

SONATA IV:

At the end of this piece, in adjusting the modern notation of first and second endings, I have moved the corona in the left hand from a double bar which separates second and first endings in the original, to the low D, so as to coincide with the corona in the right hand.

SONATA VII:

Measure 67: Repeated in Venice, Parma, and Worgan. I consider this repetition a mistake and have eliminated it.

Measure 151: Before the trill Worgan inserts an appoggiatura on A. Parma inserts one on F, connected with the trill by a slur. Venice has only the trill.

SONATA VIII:

Measure 2: Venice and Worgan have B in the alto, last quarter. Parma has D♯, which I prefer.

Measure 9: Parma gives the alto B as a whole note. I give the reading of Venice and Worgan.

Measures 38-39: In Parma the tie is placed on the soprano F♯. I have chosen the reading of Venice and Worgan, which place it on the alto B.

Measures 41 and 43: In Venice the slur embraces only the second and third quarters. In Worgan it embraces the whole measure, as also in Parma, where however it appears only in measure 43.

Measures 51 and 53: In Worgan the soprano D in the second half of the measure is preceded by an appoggiatura on E. This appoggiatura is absent in Venice and Parma.

SONATA IX:

Measure 25: The left-hand octave E on the first quarter, missing in Venice, Parma and Worgan, is inserted by me.

Measure 28: Neither Venice, Parma, nor Worgan gives a bass in this measure. I have inserted it.

Measure 49: The alto E, absent in Venice, Parma, and Worgan, is inserted by me, in order to correspond with measure 46. Only the excesses of previous editors of Scarlatti have restrained me from adding an alto D (which I frequently play) to the second half of the measure, in both measures 46 and 49.

SONATA X:

Measure 81: I have inserted the left-hand F, omitted in Venice, Parma, and Worgan.

Measures 128-129: In Worgan the soprano B♭ bears the indication, *Tremulo*, which is absent in Venice and Parma.

Measures 154, 156, 158, 162, 164, 166: On the soprano F Worgan has a trill which is absent in Venice and Parma.

SONATA XI:

Measure 60: I have inserted the soprano F, omitted in Venice.

SONATA XII:

This sonata appears twice in Venice XIV, once as number 10, and again as number 61. Neither text by itself is consistent or entirely satisfactory. The present text is a composite reading, representing my choice of the most preferable versions. I have added nothing that is not to be found in one of the two sources. I have however moved the coronas that appear on the final double bar only in Venice XIV 10 to the preceding rests, in order to correspond to the first ending of the first half.

Measures 13-14: The tenor C of measure 13, and the bass F and G of measure 14 are written in Venice XIV 61 in quarter notes followed by a wavy line. In Venice XIV 10 they are written as half notes. In order to eliminate the unfamiliar wavy lines, I might have translated parallel passages accordingly, but I have preferred to retain the indefinite notation which Scarlatti evidently used to indicate an overlapping, super-legato style of playing, in which chord tones are intended to be sustained, regardless of part-writing.

SONATA XIII:

Measure 38: Although neither Venice, Parma, nor Worgan gives a sharp for the soprano G, I have inserted it in the text.

SONATA XIV:

Measures 59-62 are omitted in Venice but present in Parma and Worgan.

SONATA XVI:

Measure 84: The soprano A has a flat in Worgan, but not in Venice or Parma. I have adopted it out of consistency with measure 17, in which all three sources give an A♭.

SONATA XVII:

Measures 28 and 56: The orthography of the indications for *tremulo* is taken from Worgan, as more complete than Venice. Parma does not mention the *tremulo* in measure 56.

Measure 88: On the bass E Parma has a trill which is not in Venice and Worgan.

Measure 95: Parma and Worgan have a trill in the right hand. Venice omits it.

SONATA XVIII:

The tempo indication in Venice is *Allegrissimo*. In Worgan it is *Allegro*. In Parma there is none.

Measure 11: In the right hand on the B of the last beat Worgan has a trill which does not appear in Venice or Parma.

Measure 15: The two tenor dotted half notes are tied in Worgan, but not in Venice or Parma.

Measure 16: Worgan gives the right hand as follows: Venice and Parma agree in the text I have chosen.

Measure 50: In the last quarter in the right hand Venice and Worgan omit the C♯, D, and E, and tie the A to the preceding. I give the Parma version.

Measure 58 has been added by me to fill out the time necessary for the repeat.

SONATA XIX:

In Venice the tempo indication is *Cantabile*. In Parma and Fitzwilliam it is *Andante*.

Measures 29 and 31, 69 and 71: Only Parma has the indication, *tremulo*.

Measure 31: The last quarter note in the right hand is D in Venice, B in Parma and Fitz-william.

Measure 52: In the last two beats Venice adds a bass A (absent in Parma and Fitzwilliam) a third below the C♯. I have omitted it.

Measure 56: I have slightly corrected the version of the first beat given in Venice as

. Parma gives it as . , and Fitzwilliam as

. Exact observance by the player of such often imprecisely notated rhyth-mic values is obviously not intended.

Measure 63: In the last chord of the left hand Parma and Fitzwilliam have an A instead of the B which appears in Venice and which seems to me correct.

Measure 77: Venice, Parma, and Fitzwilliam all resolutely omit the E which one might be tempted to add to the soprano.

SONATA XX:

Measures 7-8: The slurs on the appoggiaturas are so placed in Venice that they look like ties to the preceding notes. These are not present in Parma or Fitzwilliam. In similar cases, how-ever, I have found that a comparison of manuscripts showed that such slurs were intended to connect the appoggiatura with the main note, and not to tie it to the preceding.

SONATA XXI:

From the inconsistent orthography of both Venice and Parma for the *tremulo* I have chosen that which is most complete. In measure 68 the *tremulo* is omitted in Venice, but present in Parma.

SONATA XXII:

In the last measure Worgan has an appoggiatura on C♯ in the right hand. It is absent in Venice and Parma.

SONATA XXIII:

Measure 9:: It is possible that the omission of a sharp before the bass G in both Venice and Parma was accidental. It was not in the key signature, since both manuscripts here indicate the key of A major with only two sharps.

SONATA XXIV:

Measures 5 and 7: Venice has the trill on B, while Parma has it on C♯. I have chosen the Parma version.

Measures 70 and 147: Both Venice and Parma drop out the bass.

SONATA XXV:

Measures 14-15: These measures are repeated in Parma but not in Venice. I consider their repetition a mistake.

SONATA XXVII:

To anyone familiar with 18th-century notation of dotted rhythms it is clear that throughout this piece all eighth-note rests are to be dotted, and that all eighth notes are to be played as sixteenths. (See for example such variants as the following: In measure 8 the first B in the tenor is an eighth note in Venice, a sixteenth note in Parma. In measure 30 the first E in the soprano is an eighth note in Venice, a sixteenth note in Parma. In measure 36 the first G in the alto is a sixteenth note in Venice, an eighth note in Parma.) Although there can be no doubt about the execution of this piece, I have not attempted to modernize its rhythmic notation. I prefer always to adhere to the principle of respecting the vagaries of 18th-century dotted notation because of the many cases other than this piece in which there is room for a divergence of opinion regarding execution.

SONATA XXVIII:

Measure 42: Parma has E♭ for the last eighth note of the alto, while Venice has A♭. I have chosen the Parma reading.

SONATA XXIX:

Measures 24 and 55: I reproduce the discrepancy between these two measures which is present in both Venice and Parma.

SONATA XXX:

Measure 120: In Venice the bass is F; in Parma it is E♭. After some hesitation I have adopted the Parma reading. I am tempted however to play F as the bass in measure 119.

Measures 131-135: Neither in Venice nor Parma is there a flat for the tenor D. I have inserted it in the present text.

SONATA XXXII:

The Parma notation of ornaments is used, except for measures 12 and 182 in which I adopt the trill sign ~ from Venice rather than the *tr* in Parma.

Measure 53: Both Venice and Parma omit the bass. I have supplied it from the parallel passage.

Measures 116 and 119: Both Venice and Parma omit the bass. The B is my insertion.

SONATA XXXVII:

Measure 105: The alto, last quarter note, is F♯ in Venice, G in Parma. I have chosen the Venice reading.

Measure 134: Both Venice and Parma give the bass as D♯, E, surely mistakenly. I have adopted the reading of parallel passages.

SONATA XXXIX:

Measure 14: Venice and Parma give the trill on the D♯. I have moved it to the preceding E.

Measures 84-85: The position of the tie is unclear in both Venice and Parma. Given the notation in both manuscripts of the soprano as a half note and of the alto as a dotted half note, the tie can apply only to the tenor. I insert however a conjectural quarter note on the alto C, tied over to the following measure.

SONATA XLI:

Measures 4 and 10: The E of the left-hand chord is present in Parma but not in Venice.

SONATA XLII:

Measures 10 and 12: There is no sharp for the bass F, either in Venice or Parma.

Measures 45-46: Between these two measures in both Venice and Parma appears a measure duplicating measure 38. Since it is an obvious mistake, I have suppressed it.

Measure 103: Both Venice and Parma have D on the soprano first beat. In accordance with the parallel passage I have altered it to B.

SONATA XLIII:

Measures 8-9, 10-11, 12-13: In neither Venice nor Parma is the length of the slur easily discernible. It might be interpreted to extend only from B♭ to B♭, or possibly to extend from the first A to the second B♭.

SONATA XLV:

The measures before and after the double bar in the middle read in both Venice and Parma

as . I have altered them as given in my text.

Measure 113: Venice has E in the tenor of the first beat, but Parma has D. I have chosen the Parma reading.

SONATA XLVI:

Measure 24: Both Venice and Parma clearly have C♯ in the right hand. I consider it a mistake and have altered it to C♮.

Measure 87: Both Venice and Parma have G as the first note in the bass, certainly mistakenly. I have altered it to F.

SONATA XLVII:

Measure 27: The soprano is a whole note in Venice, but in Parma it consists of two half notes. I have chosen the Venice reading.

Measures 35-36: The left-hand chords are missing in both Venice and Parma. I have inserted them.

Measures 73 and 148: Both hands have a whole note in Venice and Parma. I have altered it to a dotted half note. For further consistency of notation I have eliminated from measure 73 the quarter note rest which appears in both Venice and Parma at the beginning of the second half.

Measures 112-115: Venice and Parma both mistakenly give the soprano as A. I read G. Venice makes a similar mistake in measures 145 and 147, reading F, whereas Parma reads G. The copyist must have been confused by the unaccustomed leger lines.

SONATA XLIX:

The notation of ornaments is confused in both Venice and Parma. I have adopted a reasonably consistent notation based on the preponderance of cases in Venice.

Measure 2: I give the slurs literally as they appear in both Venice and Parma, but I suspect that the second slur should extend over the entire last half of the measure.

Measure 33: The D's in the left hand are missing in both Venice and Parma. I have inserted them.

Measure 45: Both Venice and Parma have ♩ ♫♫ . I correct it to ♩ ♫♫ , to match measure 39.

Measure 81: The last quarter note in the soprano is D in both Venice and Parma. I have adopted it, but is it intentional? Should it be C♯?

Measure 84: Both Venice and Parma have ♩♩ ♫♫♫. I alter it, however, to ♫♫♫.

SONATA L:

Measure 20: The alto B is a dotted quarter note in both Venice and Parma. Its repetition in measure 24 is dotted in Parma but not in Venice.

Measure 66: The C in the left-hand chord on the third quarter is omitted in both Venice and Parma.

SONATA LI:

Measures 12 and 15: In both Venice and Parma the sharps are omitted for the alto G.

SONATA LIII:

Measure 71: The alto G is missing in both Venice and Parma. I have inserted it.

SONATA LIV:

Measure 20: In both Venice and Parma the bass G on the second quarter is omitted. I have inserted it.

Measure 29: The soprano for the first half of the measure reads ♩ ♪♫♫ in Venice; ♩ ♪♫♫ in Parma, without the dot. I read ♩ ♪♩.♫♫ .

Measure 31: The second quarter of the measure in the alto reads C in Parma, D in Venice. I have chosen the Venice reading.

SONATA LV:

Measure 4: The third eighth note in the soprano reads D in Venice, F in Parma. I have chosen the Parma version.

Measures 11-12: Missing in Parma, but present in Venice.

Measure 65: The trill sign in the right hand is placed before the alto in both Venice and Parma, despite the fact that it would appear to belong in the soprano.

SONATA LVI:

In Parma, where this sonata precedes Sonata LV, appears the annotation, "La que sigue se debe tañer primero." (The following should be played first.)

SONATA LVII:

The Venice notation of appoggiaturas is used, except for measure 36, in which I adopt the Parma reading as more consistent.

Measure 19: In both Venice and Parma an A appears a second above the G in the left hand on the second quarter of the measure. I consider it a mistake, and have omitted it.

Measure 79: In both Venice and Parma the natural is omitted for the soprano G.

SONATA LVIII:

Measures 19-20, 23-24, 29-30, etc.: The arrangement of stems is mine. In the Venice and Parma manuscripts the stems of the two upper voices point up.

Measure 33: I have inserted the soprano F which is missing in both Venice and Parma.

Measure 141: I have inserted the low C, which is missing in both Venice and Parma.

SONATA LIX:

Measure 11: In Parma there is a flat only before the first bass D. It is neither confirmed nor cancelled for the two subsequent D's.

Measure 30: In Parma there is a flat only before the first bass G. It is neither confirmed nor cancelled before the second.

SONATA LX:

Measures 11-12: In Parma the trill appears to be wrongly placed on the last note of measure 11. In accordance with its context I have moved it to the first note of measure 12.